# *humility*

## ANDREW MURRAY

# BOOKS BY ANDREW MURRAY

*The Believer's Prayer Life*
*The Believer's School of Prayer*
*The Believer's Secret of Holiness*
*The Blood of Christ*
*Divine Healing*
*Humility*
*Mighty Is Your Hand* (edited by David Hazard)
*The Ministry of Intercessory Prayer*
*The Path to Holiness*
*Raising Your Child to Love God*
*The Spirit of Christ*
*Waiting on God*

# humility

## ANDREW MURRAY

BETHANYHOUSE
Minneapolis, Minnesota

*Humility: The Journey Toward Holiness*
Andrew Murray

Published by Bethany House Publishers
A Ministry of Bethany Fellowship International
11400 Hampshire Avenue South
Bloomington, Minnesota 55438
www.bethanyhouse.com

Printed in the United States of America by
Bethany Press International, Bloomington, Minnesota 55438

**Library of Congress Cataloging-in-Publication Data**

Murray, Andrew, 1828–1917.
    Humility : the journey toward holiness / by Andrew Murray.
      p.  cm.
    ISBN 0-7642-2560-X
    1. Humility—Christianity.  I. Title.
    BV4647.H8   M87   2001
    241'.4—dc21                         2001003786

ANDREW MURRAY was born in South Africa in 1828. After receiving his education in Scotland and Holland, he returned to South Africa and spent many years as both pastor and missionary. He was a staunch advocate of biblical Christianity. He is best known for his many devotional books.

*Lord Jesus,*
*may our holiness be*
*perfect humility.*
*Let your perfect humility*
*be our holiness.*

# contents

# *foreword*

The words in this book changed my life forever. There is no other way to say it. Some ten years ago I stumbled upon an old version of this long-lost treasure, hidden under a pile of ninety-nine-cent books on a liquidation table. At the time, I had so many misconceptions about humility. For one thing, I confused it with self-loathing. Humility is not the same as beating yourself up or letting other people put you down. Humility is not the same as low self-esteem and it's not the opposite of confidence. In fact, the truly humble person walks with absolute confidence, knowing that we are simply empty vessels through whom God wants to accomplish his work. When we understand true humility, we understand that it's not about us at all. It's about God. That's a tremendously freeing realization.

No writer has had more impact on my understanding of what it takes to become a vessel God can use than Andrew

Murray. No writer has ever drawn me nearer to God than Andrew Murray. He writes with the gentle heart of the Father. The healing touch of Jesus flows from the tip of his pen. And the life-changing power of the Holy Spirit pulsates through every word.

It's my fervent hope that this book will become a constant companion to thousands of believers. That it will occupy a special place—on your nightstand, desk, or coffee table—right next to your Bible. I urge you to prayerfully undertake a careful reading of *Humility*. I believe it will open your eyes to a whole new way of living, as God, the Almighty Three-in-One, speaks to you very personally through the pages set before you now.

His Vessel,
Donna Partow
Author, *Becoming a Vessel
God Can Use*

# *preface*

There are three great motivations to humility: it becomes us as creatures; it becomes us as sinners; and it becomes us as saints. Humility is first seen in the angels, in man before the Fall, and in Jesus as the Son of Man. In our fallen state, humility points us to the only way by which we can return to our rightful place as creatures. As Christians, the mystery of grace teaches us that as we lose ourselves in the overwhelming greatness of redeeming love, humility becomes to us the consummation of everlasting blessedness.

It is common in Christian teaching to find the second aspect taught almost exclusively. Some have gone so far as to say that we must keep on sinning in order to remain humble! Others have thought that the strength of self-condemnation is the secret of humility. As a result, the Christian life has suffered where believers have not been guided to see that even in our relationships as creatures, nothing is more natural and beautiful and blessed than to be nothing in order that God may be everything. It needs to be made clear that it is not sin that humbles but grace. It is the soul occupied with God in His wonderful glory as Creator and Redeemer that will truly take the lowest place before Him.

In these meditations I have, for more than one reason, almost exclusively directed our attention to the humility that becomes us as creatures. It is not only because the connection between humility and sin is so commonly taught but also because I believe that for the fullness of the Christian life it is indispensable that prominence be given to the other aspect. If Jesus is to be our example in His lowliness, we need to understand the principles in which this quality is rooted and where we find the common ground to stand with Him. If we are to be humble not only before God but toward men, and if humility is to be our joy, we must see that it is not only the mark of shame because of sin, but apart from sin, it is being clothed with the very beauty and blessedness of Jesus. We will see that just as Jesus found glory in taking the form of a servant, so when He said to us, "Whoever wants to become great among you must be your servant" (Matthew 20:26), He was teaching us the truth that there is nothing so divine as being the servant and helper of all. The faithful servant who recognizes his position finds real pleasure in supplying the wants of the master or his guests. When we realize that humility is something infinitely deeper than contrition, and accept it as our participation in the life of Jesus, we will begin to learn that it is our true nobility, and that to prove it in being servants of all is the highest fulfillment of our destiny as men created in the image of God.

When I look back upon my own Christian experience, or at the church of Christ as a whole, I am amazed at how little humility is seen as the distinguishing feature of discipleship. In our preaching and in our living, in our daily interaction in our families and in our social life, as well as fellowship with other Christians, how easy it is to see that humility is not esteemed the cardinal virtue, the root from which grace can grow and the one indispensable condition of true fellowship with Jesus. The fact that it is possible for anyone to say of those who claim to seek holiness that the profession has not been accompanied with increasing humility, is a loud call to all earnest Christians, whatever truth there be in the charge, to prove that meekness and lowliness of heart are the chief marks by which they who follow the Lamb of God are to be known.

# chapter one
## humility: the glory of the creature

---

"Humility is the proper estimate of oneself."

CHARLES SPURGEON

They lay their crowns before the throne and say: "You are worthy, our Lord and God, to receive glory and honor and power, for you created all things, and by your will they were created and have their being."

Revelation 4:10–11

When God created the universe, it was with the objective of making those he created partakers of His perfection and blessedness, thus showing forth the glory of His love and wisdom and power. God desired to reveal himself in and through His creatures by communicating to them as much of His own goodness and glory as they were capable of receiving. But this communication was not meant to give created beings something they could possess in themselves, having full charge and access apart from Him. Rather, God as the ever-living, ever-present, ever-acting One, who upholds all things by the word of His power, and in whom all things exist, meant that the relationship of His creatures to himself would be one of unceasing, absolute dependence. As truly as God by His power once created all things, so by that same power must God every moment maintain all things. We as His creatures have not only to look back to the origin and beginning of our existence and acknowledge that we owe everything to God— our chief care, highest virtue, and only happiness, now and throughout all eternity—but we must also present ourselves as empty vessels, in which God can dwell and manifest His power and goodness.

The life God bestows is imparted not once for all but each moment by the unceasing operation of His mighty power. Humility, the place of entire dependence upon God, is from the very nature of things the first duty and the highest virtue of His creatures.

And so pride—the loss of humility—is the root of every sin and evil. It was when the now-fallen angels began to look upon themselves with self-complacency that they were led to disobedience and were cast down from the light of heaven into outer darkness. Likewise, it was when the serpent breathed the poison of his pride—the desire to be as God—into the hearts of our first parents, that they too fell from their high estate into the wretchedness to which all humankind has sunk. In heaven and on earth, pride or self-exaltation is the very gateway to hell.[1]

And so it follows that nothing can save us but the restoration of our lost humility, the original and only true relationship of the creature to its God. And so Jesus came to bring humility back to earth, to make us partakers of it, and by it to save us. In heaven He humbled himself to become a man. The humility we see in Him possessed Him in heaven; it brought Him here. Here on earth "He humbled himself and became obedient to death"; His humility gave His death its value, and so became our redemption. And now the salvation He imparts is nothing less and nothing else than a communication of His own life and death, His own disposition and spirit, His own humility, as the ground and root of His relationship with God and His redeeming work. Jesus Christ took the place and fulfilled the destiny of man as a creature by His life of perfect humility. His humility became our salvation. His salvation is our humility.

The life of those who are saved, the saints, must bear this stamp of deliverance from sin and full restoration to their original state; their whole relationship to God and to man marked by an all-pervading humility. Without this there can be no true abiding in God's presence or experience of His favor and the power of His Spirit; without this no abiding faith or love or joy or strength. Humility is the only soil in which virtue takes root; a lack of humility is the explanation of every defect and failure. Humility is not so much a virtue along with the others, but is the root of all, because it alone takes the right attitude before God and allows Him, as God, to do all.

God has so constituted us as reasonable beings that the greater the insight into the true nature or the absolute need of a command, the quicker and more complete will be our obedience to it. The call to humility has been too little regarded in the church because its true nature and importance have been too little apprehended. It is not something that we bring to God, or that He bestows; it is simply the sense of entire nothingness that comes when we see how truly God is everything. When the creature realizes that this is a place of honor, and consents to be—with his will, his mind, and his affections—the vessel in which the life and glory of God are to work and manifest themselves, he sees that humility is simply acknowledging the truth of his position as creature and yielding to God His place.

In the life of earnest Christians who pursue and profess

holiness, humility ought to be the chief mark of their uprightness. Often it is said that this is not the case. Perhaps one reason is that the teaching and example of the church has not placed the proper importance on humility. As strong as sin is a motive for it, there is one still wider and mightier influence: it is that which made the angels, Jesus himself, and the holiest saints humble. It is the first and chief mark of the relationship of the creature to God, of the Son to the Father—it is the secret of blessedness, the desire to be nothing, that allows God to be all in all.

I am sure there are many Christians who will confess that their experience has been very much like my own. I had long known the Lord without realizing that meekness and lowliness of heart are to be the distinguishing feature of the disciple, just as they were of the Master. And further, that this humility is not something that will come of itself, but that it must be made the object of special desire, prayer, faith, and practice. As we study the Word, we will see what very distinct and oft-repeated instructions Jesus gave His disciples on this point, and how slow they were to understand them.

Let us at the very outset of our meditations, then, admit that there is nothing so natural to man, nothing so insidious and hidden from our sight, nothing so difficult and dangerous as pride. And acknowledge that nothing but a very determined and persevering waiting on God will reveal how lacking we are in the grace of humility and how powerless we are to obtain what we seek. We must study the character of Christ until our souls are filled with the love and admiration of His lowliness.

We must believe that when we are broken under a sense of pride and our inability to cast it out, Jesus Christ himself will come to impart this grace as a part of His wonderful life within us.

# chapter two

## humility: the secret of redemption

---

"If you are looking for an example of humility,
look at the cross."

THOMAS AQUINAS

Your attitude should be the same as that of Christ Jesus: Who, being in very nature God, did not consider equality with God something to be grasped, but made himself nothing, taking the very nature of a servant, being made in human likeness. And being found in appearance as a man, he humbled himself and became obedient to death—even death on a cross! Therefore God exalted him to the highest place and gave him the name that is above every name.

**Philippians 2:5–9**

No tree can grow except on the root from which it sprang. Through all its existence it can only live by the life that was in the seed that gave it being. The full apprehension of this truth in its application to the first and the Second Adam cannot but help us to understand both the need and the nature of the redemption that is in Jesus.

## The Need

When the Old Serpent, who had been cast out of heaven for his pride, whose whole nature was pride, spoke temptation into Eve's ear, those words carried with them the very poison of hell. And when she listened, and yielded her desire and her will to the prospect of being like God, knowing good and evil, the poison entered into her soul, destroying forever that blessed humility and dependence upon God that would have been our everlasting inheritance and happiness. Her life and the life of the race that sprang from her became corrupted to its very root with that most terrible of all sins and curses—Satan's pride. All the wretchedness of which this world has been the scene, all its wars and bloodshed among the nations,

all its selfishness and suffering, all its vain ambitions and jeal-
ousies, all its broken hearts and embittered lives, with all its
daily unhappiness, have their origin in what this cursed
pride—our own or that of others—has brought upon us. It is
pride that made redemption necessary; it is from our pride
that we need, above everything else, to be redeemed. And our
insight into the need of redemption will largely depend upon
our knowledge of the terrible nature of the power of pride that
has entered our being.

As we have said, no tree can grow except on the root from
which it sprang. The pride that Satan brought from hell and
whispered into the life of humankind is working daily, hourly,
and with mighty power throughout the world. Men and
women suffer from it; they fear and fight and flee it; and yet
they don't always know where it has come from or how it has
gained such terrible supremacy. No wonder they don't know
how to overcome it. Pride has its root and strength in a spiritual power, outside of us as well as within us; as needful as it
is that we confess and deplore it, it is satanic in origin. If this
leads us to utter despair of ever conquering or casting it out,
it will lead us all the sooner to that supernatural power in
which alone our deliverance is to be found—the redemption
of the Lamb of God. The hopeless struggle against the workings of self and pride within us may indeed become still more
hopeless as we think of the power of darkness behind it; the
utter despair will fit us better for realizing and accepting a
power and a life outside of ourselves, the humility of heaven
brought down by the Lamb of God to cast out Satan and his
pride.

Even as we need to look to the first Adam and his failure to know the power of sin within us, we need to know the Second Adam and His power to give us the life of humility as real and abiding and enabling as was the life of pride. We have our life from and in Christ even more certainly than from and in Adam. We are to walk "rooted in him, holding fast the head from whom the whole body increases with the increase of God." The life of God that entered human nature through the Incarnation, is the root in which we are to stand and grow; it is the same almighty power that worked there, at the Cross, and onward to the Resurrection, which works daily in us. It is of utmost importance that we study to know and trust the life that has been revealed in Christ as the life that is now ours, and waits for our consent to gain possession and mastery of our whole being.

In view of this, it is important that we know who Christ is, especially the chief characteristic that is the root and essence of His character as our Redeemer. There can be but one answer: it is His humility. What is the Incarnation but His heavenly humility, His emptying himself and becoming man? What is His life on earth but humility; His taking the form of a servant? And what is His atonement but humility? "He humbled himself and became obedient to death." And what is His ascension and His glory but humility exalted to the throne and crowned with glory? "He humbled himself . . . therefore God exalted Him to the highest place." In heaven, where He was one with the Father; in His birth, His life, and His death on earth; in His return to the right hand of the Father—it is all humility. Christ is the expression of the humility of God embodied in human nature; the Eternal Love humbling itself, clothing itself in the garb of meekness and gentleness, to win and serve and save us. As the love and condescension of God makes Him the benefactor and helper and servant of all, so Jesus of necessity was the Incarnate Humility. And so He is still, in the midst of the throne, the meek and lowly Lamb of God.

If this is the root of the tree, its nature must be seen in every branch and leaf and fruit. If humility is the first, the all-inclusive grace of the life of Jesus—if humility is the secret of His atonement—then the health and strength of our spiritual life will depend entirely upon our putting this grace first and making humility the chief quality we admire in Him, the chief attribute we ask of Him, the one thing for which we sacrifice all else.[1]

Is it any wonder that the Christian life is so often weak and fruitless, when the very root of the Christian life is neglected or unknown? Is it any wonder that the joy of salvation is so little felt, when that by which Christ brings it is so seldom sought? Until a humility that rests in nothing less than the end and death of self, and which gives up all the honor of men as Jesus did to seek the honor that comes from God alone (which absolutely makes and counts itself nothing) that God may be all, that the Lord alone may be exalted—until such a humility is what we seek in Christ above our chief joy, and welcome at any price, there is very little hope of a faith that will conquer the world.

I cannot too greatly impress upon my readers the need of realizing the lack there is today of humility within Christian circles. There is so little of the meek and lowly Lamb of God in those who are called by His name. Let us consider how our lack of love, indifference to the needs and feelings of others, even sharp comments and hasty judgments that are often excused as being honest and straightforward, are thwarting the effect of the influence of the Holy Spirit on others. Manifestations of temper and touchiness and irritation, feelings of bitterness and estrangement, have their root in nothing but pride. Pride creeps in almost everywhere, and the assemblies of the saints are not exceptions. Let's ask ourselves what would be the effect if all of us were guided by the humility of Jesus, that the cry of our whole heart, night and day, would be, "Oh, for the humility of Jesus in myself and all around me!" Let us honestly fix our heart on our lack of humility—that which has been revealed in the likeness of Christ's life, in the whole character of His redemption—and realize how little we know of Christ and His salvation.

*Study* the humility of Jesus. This is the secret, the hidden root of redemption. Believe with your whole heart that Christ, whom God has given you, will enter in to dwell and work within you and make you what the Father would have you to be.

# chapter three
## humility in the life of Jesus

---

"The only hope of a decreasing self
is an increasing Christ."

F. B. Meyer

I am among you as one who serves.

Luke 22:27

In the gospel of John we have the inner life of our Lord laid open before us. Jesus spoke frequently of His relationship to the Father, of the motives by which He was guided, of His consciousness of the power and Spirit in which He acted. Though the word *humble* does not occur in Scripture, the humility of Christ is clearly revealed. We have already said that this virtue is nothing but the simple consent of the creature to let God be all, the surrender of itself to His working alone. In Jesus we see how both as the Son of God in heaven and the Son of Man on earth, He took the place of entire subordination and gave God the Father the honor and glory due Him. What He taught so often was true of himself: "He who humbles himself will be exalted" (Luke 18:14). As it is written, "He humbled himself. . . . Therefore God exalted him to the highest place" (Philippians 2:8–9).

Listen to the words our Lord speaks of His relationship to the Father and see how consistently He uses the words *not* and *nothing* of himself. The *not I* that Paul uses to express his relationship to Christ, is in the same spirit that Christ speaks of His relationship to the Father.

"The Son can do *nothing* by himself" (John 5:19).

"By myself I can do *nothing*; I judge only as I hear, and my judgment is just, for I seek *not* to please myself but him who sent me" (John 5:30).

"I do *not* accept praise from men" (John 5:41).

"For I have come down from heaven *not* to do my will" (John 6:38).

"My teaching is *not* my own" (John 7:16).

"I am *not* here on my own" (John 7:28).

"I do *nothing* on my own" (John 8:28).

"I have *not* come on my own; but he sent me" (John 8:42).

"I am *not* seeking glory for myself" (John 8:50).

"The words I say to you are *not* just my own" (John 14:10).

"These words you hear are *not* my own" (John 14:24).

These words of testimony, spoken by the Lord himself, reveal the deepest motivation of His life and work. They show how the Father was able to work His redemption through the Son. They show the state of heart that became Him as the Son of the Father. They teach us the essential nature and life of the redemption that Christ accomplished and now communicates to us. It is this: He was nothing that God might be all. He resigned himself to the Father's will and power that He might work through Him. Of His own power, His own will, His own glory, His whole mission with its works and teaching—of all this, He said, I am nothing. I have given myself to the Father to work; He is all.

This life of entire self-abnegation, of absolute submission and dependence upon the Father's will, Christ found to be the source of perfect peace and joy. He lost nothing by giving all to God. God honored His trust and did all for Him, and then exalted Him to His own right hand in glory. And because Christ humbled himself before God, and God was ever before Him, He found it possible to humble himself before men, too, and to be the Servant of all. His humility was simply the surrender of himself to God, to allow Him to do in Him what He pleased, regardless of what men might say of Him or do to Him.

It is in this state of mind, in this spirit and disposition, that the redemption of Christ has its virtue and efficacy. It is to bring us to this disposition that we are made partakers of Christ. This is the true self-denial to which our Savior calls us, the acknowledgment that self has nothing good in it, except as an empty vessel for God to fill. Its claim to be or do anything may not for a moment be allowed. It is in this, above and before everything, that the conformity to Jesus consists—the being and doing nothing of ourselves that God may be all in all.

Here we have the nature of true humility. It is because this is not understood or sought after, that our humility is so superficial and weak. We must learn of Jesus, how He is meek and lowly of heart. He teaches us where true humility begins and finds its strength—in the knowledge that it is God who works all in all, that our place is to yield to Him in perfect resignation and dependence, in full consent to be and to do nothing of ourselves. This is the life Christ came to reveal and to impart—a life to God that came through death to sin and self. If we feel that this life is too high for us and beyond our reach, it must all the more urge us to seek it in Him. It is the indwelling Christ who will live this life in us. If we long for it, let us above everything seek the secret of the knowledge of the nature of God, the secret of which every child of God is to be a witness: nothing but a vessel, a channel through which the living God can manifest the riches of His wisdom, power, and goodness. The root of all virtue and grace, of all faith and acceptable worship, is that we know that we have nothing but what we receive, and bow in deepest humility to wait upon God for it.

It was because this humility was not only a temporary sentiment awakened in Him when He thought of God but also was the spirit of His whole life, that Jesus was as humble in His relationship with men and women as He was with God. He felt himself to be the Servant of God for those whom God created and loved. As a natural consequence, He counted himself the Servant of men and women so that through Him God might do His work of love. He never for a moment sought His own honor or asserted His power to vindicate himself. His whole spirit was that of a life yielded to God. When we study the humility of Jesus as the very essence of His redemption, as the blessedness of the life of the Son of God, and as the virtue Jesus gives us if we are to have any part with Him, we will begin to comprehend how serious it is to lack humility in our lives.

Are you clothed with humility? Look at your daily life. Ask your friends about it. Begin to praise God that there is opened to you in Jesus a heavenly humility that you have hardly known and through which a heavenly blessedness you have never tasted can come.

# humility in the teaching of Jesus

---

"Humility must always be doing its work like a bee
making its honey in the hive: without humility
all will be lost."

TERESA OF AVILA

Learn from me, for I am gentle and humble in heart.

**Matthew 11:29**

---

Whoever wants to be first must be your slave—just as the Son of Man did not come to be served, but to serve.

**Matthew 20:27–28**

W e see humility in the life of Christ demonstrated in how He laid open His heart to us. Through His teaching we hear Him speak of it—how He expects His disciples to be humble as He was. Let us carefully study the passages to see how often and how earnestly He taught it: it may help us to realize what He asks of us.

1. Look at the commencement of His ministry. In the Sermon on the Mount, He opens with the Beatitudes: "Blessed are the poor in spirit, for theirs is the kingdom of heaven. Blessed are the meek, for they will inherit the earth" (Matthew 5:3, 5). The very first words of His proclamation of the kingdom of heaven reveal the open gate through which we may enter. The kingdom comes to the poor, who have nothing in themselves. The earth is for the meek, who seek nothing for themselves. The blessings of heaven and earth are for the lowly. Humility is the secret of blessing for the heavenly and the earthly life.

2. "Learn from me, for I am gentle and humble in heart, and you will find rest for your souls" (Matthew 11:29). Jesus offers himself as Teacher. He tells us both what the Spirit is and what we can learn and receive from Him. Meekness and

lowliness are the qualities He offers us; in them we will find perfect rest. Humility is our salvation.

3. The disciples had been disputing among themselves who would be the greatest in the kingdom, and had agreed to ask the Master (Luke 9:46; Matthew 18:3). He placed a child in their midst, and said, "Whoever humbles himself like this child is the greatest in the kingdom of heaven" (Matthew 18:4). "Who is the greatest in the kingdom of heaven?" The question is far-reaching. What will be the chief distinction in the heavenly kingdom? The glory of heaven, the mind of heaven, is humility. "He who is least among you all—he is the greatest" (Luke 9:48).

4. The sons of Zebedee asked Jesus if they could sit on His right hand and on His left, the highest places in the kingdom. Jesus said it was not His to give but the Father's, who would give it to those for whom it was prepared. They must not seek it or ask for it. Their thoughts must be of the cup and the baptism of humiliation. And then He added, "Whoever wants to be first must be your slave—just as the Son of Man did not come to be served, but to serve" (Matthew 20:27–28). Humility, as it is the mark of Christ, will be the one standard of glory in heaven: the lowliest is the nearest to God.

5. Speaking to the multitude and the disciples, of the Pharisees and their love of the chief seats, Christ said once again, "The greatest among you will be your servant" (Matthew 23:11). Humiliation is the only ladder to honor in God's kingdom.

6. On another occasion, in the house of a Pharisee, He spoke the parable of the guest who would be invited to come

up higher, and added, "For everyone who exalts himself will be humbled, and he who humbles himself will be exalted" (Luke 14:1–11). The demand is inexorable; there is no other way. Self-abasement alone will be exalted.

7. After the parable of the Pharisee and the Publican, Christ spoke again, "For everyone who exalts himself will be humbled, and he who humbles himself will be exalted" (Luke 18:14). In the temple and presence and worship of God, everything is worthless that is not pervaded by deep, true humility toward God and humankind.

8. After washing the disciples' feet, Jesus said, "Now that I, your Lord and Teacher, have washed your feet, you also should wash one another's feet" (John 13:14). The authority of command and example, every thought, either of obedience or conformity, makes humility the first and most essential element of discipleship.

9. At the Lord's Supper table, the disciples still disputed who should be greatest. Jesus said, "The greatest among you should be like the youngest, and the one who rules like the one who serves. . . . I am among you as one who serves" (Luke 22:26–27). The path Jesus walked, which He opened up for us, the power through which He wrought our salvation and by which He saves us, is the humility that makes us the servant of all.

How little this is preached. How seldom it is practiced. How faintly the lack of it is felt or confessed. I cannot say how few attain to some recognizable measure of likeness to Jesus in His humility. But fewer ever think of making it a distinct object of continual desire or prayer. How little the world has seen it. How scarcely it is seen in the inner circle of the church.

"Whosoever will be chief among you, let him be your servant." Oh that God would convince us that Jesus means this! We all know what the character of a faithful servant or slave implies. Devotion to the master's interests, thoughtful study and care to please him, delight in his prosperity and honor and happiness. There are servants on earth in whom these dispositions have been seen, and to whom the name of servant has never been anything but glory. To how many of us has it been a new joy in the Christian life to know that we may yield ourselves as servants, as slaves to God, and to find that His service is our highest liberty—the freedom from sin and self? We need to learn another lesson—that Jesus calls us to be servants of one another, and that as we accept it heartily, this service will be a most blessed one, a new and fuller deliverance from sin and self. At first it may appear hard—this is because of the pride that still counts itself something. If once we learn that to be nothing before God is the glory of the creature, the spirit of Jesus, the joy of heaven, we shall welcome with our whole heart the discipline we may have in serving even those who try or annoy us. When our own heart is set upon this true sanctification, we will study each word of Jesus on self-abasement with new zeal, and no place will be too low, no stooping too far, and no service too mean or too long if we may but share and prove the fellowship with Him who said, "I am among you as one who serves" (Luke 22:27).

Here is the path to the higher life. It is the lowest path! This was what Jesus said to the disciples who were thinking of being great in the kingdom and of sitting on His right hand and His left. Ask not for exaltation. That is God's work. See that you humble yourselves, and take no place before God or man but that of a servant. That is your work; let that be your one purpose and prayer. God is faithful. Just as water seeks and fills the lowest place, so the moment God finds the creature empty, His glory and power flow in to exalt and to bless. He that humbles himself—that must be our one aim—shall be exalted; that is God's aim. By His mighty power and in His great love He will do it.

People sometimes speak of humility and meekness as something that would rob us of what is noble and bold. Oh, that all would realize that this is the nobility of the kingdom of heaven, that this is the royal spirit that the King of heaven displayed, that this is godlike, to humble oneself and to become the servant of all! This is the path to the gladness and the glory of Christ's presence in us, of His power resting upon us.

Jesus, the meek and lowly One, calls us to learn of Him the path to God. Let us study the words we have been reading until our heart is filled with the thought: *My one need is humility*. And let us believe that what He shows He gives, and what He is He imparts. As the meek and lowly One, He will come into and dwell within the longing heart.

## chapter five

# humility in the disciples of Jesus

---

"God created the world out of nothing, and as long as we are nothing, He can make something out of us."

MARTIN LUTHER

The greatest among you should be like the youngest, and the one who rules like the one who serves.

**Luke 22:26**

We have studied humility in the person and teaching of Jesus; now we will look for it in the circle of His chosen companions—the twelve apostles. If we see a lack of humility in the disciples, and a contrast between Christ and men is brought out more clearly, it will help us to appreciate the mighty change that Pentecost brought and prove how real our participation can be in the triumph of Christ's humility over the pride Satan breathed into humankind.

In the texts quoted from the teaching of Jesus, we have seen the occasions on which the disciples proved how much they lacked the grace of humility. Once they were disputing about who should be the greatest. Another time the sons of Zebedee, with their mother, had asked for the first places—the seats on the right hand and the left of Jesus in glory. And later on, at the Last Supper, there was a contention again about who should be counted the greatest. This is not to say that there were not moments when they did humble themselves before the Lord. Peter cried out, "Go away from me, Lord; I am a sinful man!" (Luke 5:8). On another occasion, the disciples fell down and worshiped Him when He stilled the storm. But such infrequent expressions of humility only emphasize the general habit of their minds, as shown in the natural and spontaneous revelations of the place and power of self. The study of the meaning of their behavior will teach us some important lessons.

*First, is the fact that there may be the enthusiastic and active practice of Christianity while humility is still sadly lacking.* The disciples had a fervent attachment to Jesus. They had forsaken all to follow Him. The Father had revealed to them that He was the Christ of God. They believed in Him, they loved Him, and they obeyed His commandments. When others fell away, they remained faithful to Him. They were ready to die with Him. But deeper than all of this devotion was the existence of an inner power of sin and selfishness. This power had to be dealt with before they could be witnesses of the power of Jesus to save. It is so with all of us. We may find professors and ministers, evangelists and Christian workers, missionaries and teachers, in whom the gifts of the Spirit are many and manifest, and who are the channels of blessing to multitudes, but of whom, when tested, or close interpersonal relationships reveal their true characters, it is only too evident that the grace of humility, as an abiding characteristic, is rarely to be seen. All of this tends to confirm the reality that humility is one of the chief and highest virtues, one of the most difficult to attain, and one to which our first and greatest efforts ought to be directed. Humility is a virtue that only comes in power when the fullness of the Spirit makes us partakers of the indwelling Christ and He lives within us.

*Second, is the reality that external teaching and personal effort are powerless to conquer pride or create the meek and lowly heart in a person.* For three years the disciples had been in the training school of Jesus. He had told them what the main lesson was that He wished to teach them: "Learn from me, for I am gentle and humble in heart" (Matthew 11:29). Time after time He had spoken to them, to the Pharisees, and to the multitudes, of humility as the only path to the glory of God. He had not only lived before them as the Lamb of God in His divine humility but He had also more than once unfolded to them the inmost secret of His life: "The Son of Man did not come to be served, but to serve" (Matthew 20:28); "I am among you as one who serves" (Luke 22:27). He had washed their feet and told them to follow His example. But all was to little avail. At the Last Supper there was still contention as to who should be greatest. They had doubtless tried to learn His lessons, and firmly resolved not to grieve Him again. But all was in vain. To teach them and us the lesson that no outward instruction, not even of Christ himself; no argument, however convincing; no sense of the beauty of humility, however deep; no personal resolve or effort, however sincere and earnest, can cast out pride. When Satan casts out Satan, it is only that he might enter afresh in a mightier, subtler power. Nothing works but this: that the new nature in its divine humility be revealed in power to take the place of the old—to become our true nature.

*Third, is the revelation that it is only by the indwelling of Christ in His divine humility that we can become truly humble.* We have our pride from Adam; we must have our humility from Christ. Pride rules in us with incredible power; it is ourselves, our very nature. Humility must become ours in the same way; it must be our true selves, our very nature. As natural and easy as it has been to be proud, it must become natural for us to be humble. The promise is "Where sin abounded, grace did abound more exceedingly." All Christ's teaching of His disciples, and all their vain efforts, were the needful preparation for His entering into them in divine power, to give and be in them what He had taught them to desire. In His death, He destroyed the power of the devil. He put away sin and produced an everlasting redemption. In His resurrection He received from the Father an entirely new life, the life of man in the power of God, capable of being communicated to men, and entering and renewing and filling their lives with His divine power. In His ascension He received the Spirit of the Father, through whom He might do what He could not do while upon earth—make himself one with those He loved, actually live their life for them, so that they could live before the Father in a humility like His own. On Pentecost He came and took possession of the church. The work of preparation and conviction, the awakening of desire and hope that His teaching brought about, was perfected by the mighty change of Pentecost. The lives and the epistles of James and Peter and John bear witness that all was changed, and that the spirit of the meek and suffering Jesus had taken possession of them.

Is this new information? There may be some readers who have never given particular thought to the subject, and therefore do not yet realize its immense importance as a question for the church. There are others who have felt condemned for their lack of humility, and have made great efforts, only to fail and to be discouraged. Still others may be able to give joyful testimony of spiritual blessing and power, yet there has never been conviction concerning the lack in those around them. Some may be able to witness to the Lord's deliverance and victory in this area, but realize how much they still need and may expect from the fullness of Jesus. To whatever class you belong, may I urge the pressing need to seek a deeper conviction of the unique place that humility holds in the life of every believer. Let us consider how far the disciples were advanced while this grace was still lacking, and let us pray that other gifts may not so satisfy us that we never grasp the fact that the absence of humility is no doubt the reason why the power of God cannot do its mighty work. It is only where we, like the Son, truly know and show that we can do nothing of ourselves that God will do everything.

It is when the truth of the indwelling Christ takes the place it deserves in the experience of believers that the church will put on her beautiful garment and humility will be seen in her teachers and members as the beauty of holiness.

## chapter six
# humility in daily life

---

"The more humble a man is in himself, the more obedient toward God, the wiser will he be in all things, and the more shall his soul be at peace."

THOMAS À KEMPIS

For anyone who does not love his brother, whom he has seen, cannot love God, whom he has not seen.

**1 John 4:20**

It is a solemn thought that our love for God is measured by our everyday relationships with others. Except as its validity is proven in standing the test of daily life with our fellowmen, our love for God may be found to be a delusion. It is easy to think that we humble ourselves before God, but our humility toward others is the only sufficient proof that our humility before God is real. To be genuine, humility must abide in us and become our very nature. True humility is to be made of no reputation—as did Christ. In God's presence, humility is not a posture we assume for a time—when we think of Him or pray to Him—but the very spirit of our life. It will manifest itself in all our bearing toward others. A lesson of deepest importance is that the only humility that is really ours is not the kind we try to show before God in prayer, but the kind we carry with us, and carry out, in our ordinary conduct. The seemingly insignificant acts of daily life are the tests of eternity, because they prove what spirit possesses us. It is in our most unguarded moments that we truly show who we are and what we are made of. To know a truly humble person, you must follow that one in the common course of daily life.

This is what Jesus taught. He gave them an example when

He washed their feet. He taught His lessons of humility by demonstration. Humility before God is nothing if it is not proven in humility before others.

It is so in the teaching of Paul. To the Romans he writes, "Honor one another *above yourselves*" (Romans 12:10); "Do not be proud, but be willing to associate with *people of low position*. Do not be conceited" (Romans 12:16). And to the Corinthians: "Love"—and there is no love without humility as its root—"does not boast, it is not proud.... It is not self-seeking, it is not easily angered" (1 Corinthians 13:4–5). To the Galatians: "Serve *one another* in love (Galatians 5:13). Let us not become conceited, provoking and envying *each other*" (Galatians 5:26). To the Ephesians, immediately after the three wonderful chapters on the heavenly life, he said, "Live a life ... completely humble and gentle; be patient, bearing with *one another* in love" (Ephesians 4:1–2); "Always giving thanks.... Submit to *one another* out of reverence for Christ" (Ephesians 5:20–21). To the Philippians: "Do nothing out of selfish ambition or vain conceit, but in humility consider *others* better than yourselves" (Philippians 2:3). "Your attitude should be the same as that of Christ Jesus: "Who ... made himself nothing, taking the very nature of a servant ... he humbled himself" (Philippians 2:5–8). And to the Colossians: "Clothe yourselves with compassion, kindness, humility, gentleness and patience. Bear with *each other* and forgive whatever grievances you may have against *one another*. Forgive as the Lord forgave you" (Colossians 3:12). It is in our relationships with one another, in our treatment of each other, that true lowliness of mind and a heart of humility are seen. Our humility before God has no value except as it prepares us to reveal the humility of Jesus to our fellowmen. Let us study humility in daily life in light of these words.

The humble person seeks at all times to live up to the rule "Honor one another above yourselves; serve one another; consider others better than yourselves; submit to one another." The question is often asked how we can count others better than ourselves when we see that they are far below us in wisdom, in holiness, in natural gifts, or in grace received. The question proves at once how little we understand what real lowliness of mind is. True humility comes when before God we see ourselves as nothing, have put aside self, and let God be all. The soul that has done this, and can say, "I have lost myself in finding you," no longer compares itself with others. It has given up forever any thought of self in God's presence; it meets its fellowmen as one who is nothing and seeks nothing for itself; who is a servant of God and for His sake is a servant of all. A faithful servant may be wiser than his master and yet retain the true spirit and posture of a servant. The humble man looks upon every child of God, the most weak and unworthy, and honors him and prefers him as a son of the King. The spirit of Him who washed the disciples' feet makes it a joy to be the least, to be servants of one another.

The humble person feels no jealousy or envy. He can praise God when others are preferred and blessed before him. He can hear others praised and himself forgotten, because in God's presence he has learned to say with Paul, "I am nothing." He has received the spirit of Jesus, who pleased not himself and sought not His own honor as the spirit of his life.

Amid temptations to impatience and irritableness, to hard thoughts and sharp words that come in response to the failings and sins of fellow-Christians, the humble person carries the oft-repeated injunction in his heart and shows it in his life: "Forbearing one another, and forgiving one another, even as the Lord forgave you." He has learned that in putting on the Lord Jesus he puts on the heart of compassion, kindness, humility, meekness, and long-suffering. Jesus has taken the place of self, and it is not an impossibility to forgive as Jesus forgave. His humility does not consist merely in thoughts or words of self-depreciation, but, as Paul puts it, in "a heart of humility," the sweet and lowly gentleness recognized as the mark of the Lamb of God.

In striving after the higher experiences of the Christian life, the believer is often in danger of seeking the more visible virtues, such as joy, boldness, zeal, contempt of the world, self-sacrifice—even the old Stoics taught and practiced these—rather than the gentler graces, those which are more distinctly connected with Jesus' cross and death to self: poverty of spirit, meekness, humility, lowliness. Therefore, let us put on a heart of compassion, kindness, humility, meekness, long-suffering; and let us prove our Christlikeness not only in our zeal for saving the lost but also in our relationships with others—forbearing and forgiving one another, even as the Lord forgave us.

Let us study the Bible portrait of the most humble man that ever lived—the Lord Jesus. And let us ask our brethren, and the world, whether they recognize in us the likeness to the original. Let us be content with nothing less than taking each of these texts as the promise of what God will work in us, as the revelation of what the Spirit of Jesus will put within us. Allow each failure and shortcoming to only the more quickly turn us to the meek and lowly Lamb of God in the assurance that where He is enthroned in the heart, His humility and gentleness will be the streams of living water that flow from within us. George Foxe said, "I knew Jesus, and He was very precious to my soul, but I found something in me that would not keep sweet and patient and kind. I did what I could to keep it down, but it was there. I besought Jesus to do something for me, and when I gave Him my will, He came to my heart, and took out all that would not be sweet, all that would not be kind, all that would not be patient, and then He shut the door."

Once again, let me repeat what I have said before. I feel deeply that we have very little concept of what the church suffers as a result of its lack of humility—the self-abasement that makes room for God to prove His power. A Christian who was acquainted with mission stations of various societies, expressed his deep sorrow that in some cases the spirit of love and forbearance was sadly lacking. Men and women who could choose their own circle of friends, joined together in fellowship with those of contrary opinions, making it difficult to bear and to love and to keep the unity of the Spirit in the bond of peace. And those who should have been encouragers became a hindrance to the work. It appeared the lack of humility was the cause of much of the difficulty. Humility always seeks, like Jesus, to be the servant, the helper, and the comforter of others, even to the lowest and most unworthy.

Why is it that those who have joyfully given themselves up for Christ find it so hard to give themselves up for fellow Christians? It seems that the church has failed to teach its people the importance of humility—that it is the first of the virtues, the best of all the graces and powers of the Spirit. It has failed to show that a Christlike humility is what is needed and is also in the realm of possibility. But let us not be discouraged. Rather, let the discovery of the lack of this grace stir us up to greater expectation from God. Let us look upon everyone who tries us as God's means of grace, God's instrument for our purification, for our exercise of the humility of Jesus. May we have true faith in the sufficiency of God and admit to the inefficiency of self, that by God's power we will serve one another in love.

*chapter seven*

# humility and holiness

---

"It is no great thing to be humble when you are
brought low; but to be humble when you are praised
is a great and rare achievement."

BERNARD OF CLAIRVAUX

All day long I have held out my hands to an obstinate people . . . who say, "Keep away; don't come near me, for I am too sacred for you!"

**Isaiah 65:2, 5**

We speak of the holiness movement in our times and praise God for it. We hear a great deal of seekers after holiness and professors of holiness, of holiness teaching and holiness meetings. The blessed truths of holiness in Christ and holiness by faith are being emphasized as never before. The great test of whether the holiness we profess to seek or to attain is truth and life will be whether it is manifest in the increasing humility it produces. In the individual, humility is the one thing needed to allow God's holiness to dwell in and shine through him or her. In Jesus—the Holy One of God, who makes us holy—divine humility was the secret of His life, His death, and His exaltation. The one infallible test of our holiness will be our humility before God and others. Humility is the bloom and the beauty of holiness.

The chief mark of counterfeit holiness is its lack of humility. Every seeker after holiness needs to be on his guard lest unconsciously what was begun in the spirit is perfected in the flesh, and pride creep in where its presence is least expected. Two men went into the temple to pray: the one a Pharisee, the other a tax collector. There was no place or position so sacred that the Pharisee could not enter there. Pride can lift its head in the very temple of God and make His worship the scene of its self-exaltation. Since the time Christ so exposed his pride, the Pharisee has put on the garb of the tax collector. The confessor of deep sinfulness and the professor of highest holiness must both be on watch. Just when we are most anxious to have our heart be the temple of God, we will find the two men coming to pray. And the tax collector will find that his danger is not from the Pharisee beside him, who despises him, but the Pharisee within, who commends and exalts himself. In God's temple, when we think we are in the holy place, in the presence of His holiness, let us beware of pride. "One day the angels came to present themselves before the Lord, and Satan also came with them" (Job 1:6).

"God, I thank you that I am not like other men, or even like this tax collector" (Luke 18:11). It is in the thanksgiving that we render to God or the confession that God has done it all, that self finds cause for complacency. Yes, even when the language of penitence and trust in God's mercy alone is heard, the Pharisee may take up the note of praise and in thanking God be congratulating himself. Pride can clothe itself in the garments of praise or of penitence. Even though the words "I am not as other men" are rejected and condemned, their spirit may too often be found in our feelings and language toward our fellow worshipers and fellowmen. If you wonder if this is so, listen to the way Christians speak of one another. How little of the meekness and gentleness of Jesus is seen. It is seldom remembered that deep humility must be the keynote of what we say of ourselves or of each other. There are countless assemblies of saints, mission conventions, societies, or committees, where the harmony has been disturbed and the work of God hindered because men who are counted saints are touchy and impatient, self-defensive and self-assertive to the point of sharp judgments and unkind words. They do not reckon others better than themselves, and their holiness has little meekness in it.

" 'Me' is a most exacting person, requiring the best seat and the highest place for itself, and feeling grievously wounded if its claim is not recognized. Most of the quarrels among Christian workers arise from the clamoring of this gigantic 'me.' How few of us understand the true secret of taking our seats in the lowest rooms."*

In their spiritual history, men may have had times of great humbling and brokenness, but what a different thing this is from being clothed with humility, from having a humble spirit, from having that lowliness of mind in which each counts himself the servant of others and so shows forth the mind that was in Jesus Christ.

Our text is a parody on holiness! Jesus the Holy One is the humble One: the holiest will always be the humblest. There is none holy but God: we have as much holiness as we have God. And according to what we have of God will be our real humility, because humility is nothing but the disappearance of self in the vision that God is all. The holiest will be the humblest. Though the barefaced boasting Jew of the days of Isaiah is not often to be found—our manners have taught us not to speak that way—how often his spirit is still seen, whether in

---

*Quoting Mrs. Smith in *Everyday Religion*, n.d.

the treatment of fellow Christians or of the children of the world. In the spirit in which opinions are given, work is undertaken, and faults are exposed, how often, though the garb be that of the tax collector, the voice is still that of the Pharisee: "God, I thank you that I am not like other men" (Luke 18:11).

Is there such humility still to be found that men count themselves "less than the least of all saints," the servants of all? "Love . . . does not boast, it is not proud. . . . It is not self-seeking" (1 Corinthians 13:4–5). Where the spirit of love is shed abroad in the heart, where the divine nature comes to full birth, and where Christ the meek and lowly Lamb of God is truly formed within, there comes the power of a perfect love that forgets itself and finds its blessedness in blessing others. Where this love enters, God enters. And where God has come in His power and revealed himself, the vessel becomes nothing. This is the condition in which true humility can be displayed toward others. The presence of God is not dependent upon times and seasons, but upon a soul ready to do His will and forget itself.

Let all teachers of holiness, whether in the pulpit or on the platform, and all seekers after holiness, whether in the closet or the convention, take warning: There is no pride so dangerous, so subtle and insidious, as the pride of holiness. It is not that a man ever says, or even thinks, "Stay away. I am too sacred for you!" The thought would be considered ludicrous. But unconsciously there can develop a private habit of soul that feels complacency in its attainments and cannot help but see how far it is ahead of others. It isn't always seen in self-assertion or self-praise, but in the absence of self-denial and modesty that reveals a lack of the mark of the soul that has seen the glory of God (Job 42:5–6; Isaiah 6:5). It is a tone, a way of speaking of oneself or others, in which those who have the gift of discernment cannot but recognize the power of self. Even the world with its keen eye notices it, and points to it as proof that the profession of a spiritual life does not always bear spiritual fruits. Beware, lest we make a profession of holiness, delighting in beautiful thoughts and feelings, in solemn acts of consecration and faith, while the mark of the presence of God—the disappearance of self—is obviously missing. Flee to Jesus and hide yourselves in Him until you are clothed with His humility. That alone is holiness.

## chapter eight
# humility and sin

---

"Nothing sets a person so much out of the devil's
reach as humility."

JONATHAN EDWARDS

Christ Jesus came into the world to save sinners—of whom I am the worst.

1 Timothy 1:15

Humility is often identified with penitence and contrition. As a consequence, there appears to be no way of fostering humility but by keeping the soul occupied with its sin. But I think we have learned that humility is something else and something more than being consumed with our own sinfulness. We have seen in the teaching of our Lord Jesus and the Epistles how often the virtue is mentioned without any reference to sin. In the very nature of things, in the whole relationship of the creature to the Creator, in the life of Jesus as He lived it and imparts it to us, humility is the very essence of holiness. It is the displacement of self by the enthronement of God. Where God is all, self is nothing.

But though it is this aspect of the truth I have felt especially constrained to emphasize, I hardly need to say what new depth and intensity man's sin and God's grace give to the humility of the saints. We have only to look at a man like the apostle Paul to see how throughout his life as a ransomed and a holy man, the deep consciousness of having been a sinner lived in him inextinguishably. We all know the passages in which he refers to his life as a persecutor and blasphemer: "I am *the least of the apostles* and *do not even deserve to be called an apostle*, because I persecuted the church of God. But by the grace of God I am what I am, and his grace to me was not without effect. No, I worked harder than all of them—yet not I, but the grace of God that was with me" (1 Corinthians 15:9–10, emphasis added). "Although I am *less than the least of all God's people*, this grace was given me: to preach to the Gentiles" (Ephesians 3:8). "Even though I was once *a blasphemer and a persecutor and a violent man*, I was shown mercy because I acted in ignorance and unbelief. . . . Christ Jesus came into the world to save *sinners—of whom I am the worst*" (1 Timothy 1:13, 15).

God's grace had saved Paul; God remembered his sins no more; but never could Paul forget how terribly he had sinned. The more he rejoiced in God's salvation, and the more his experience of God's grace filled him with joy unspeakable, the clearer was his consciousness that he was a saved sinner and that salvation had no meaning or sweetness except that his being a sinner made it precious and real to him personally. Never for a moment could he forget that it was a sinner God had taken up in His arms and crowned with His love.

The texts we have quoted are often appealed to as Paul's confession of sinning daily. But one has only to read them carefully in their context to see that this is not the case. They have a far deeper significance. They refer to the power of God that endures throughout eternity to keep us in awe of the humility with which the ransomed bow before the throne as those who have been washed from their sins in the blood of the Lamb. Never, even in glory, can they be any other than ransomed sinners; never for a moment in this life can God's child live in the full light of His love without feeling that the sin out of which he has been saved is his one right to grace. The humility with which first he came as a sinner acquires a new meaning when he learns how it becomes him as a creature. And again, the humility in which he was born as a creature has its deepest, richest tones in the memory of what it is to be a monument of God's redeeming love.

The true importance of what these expressions of Paul teach us comes out all the more strongly when we notice the remarkable fact that through his whole Christian journey we never find from his pen anything like confession of sin. Nowhere is there any mention of shortcoming or defect, nowhere any suggestion to his readers that he has failed in duty or sinned against the law of perfect love. On the contrary, there are passages in which he vindicates himself in language that appeals to a faultless life before God and men. "You are witnesses, and so is God, of how holy, righteous and blameless we were among you who believed" (1 Thessalonians 2:10). "This is our boast: Our conscience testifies that we have conducted ourselves in the world, and especially in our relations with you, in the holiness and sincerity that are from God" (2 Corinthians 1:12). This is not an ideal or an aspiration; it is an admission of what his actual life had been. However we may account for this absence of confession of sin, all will admit that it must point to a life in the power of the Holy Spirit such as is seldom realized or expected in our day.

The point I wish to emphasize is this: the very fact of the absence of such confession of sin only gives more strength to the truth that it is not in daily sinning that the secret of humility is found, but rather in the position of dependence upon the grace of God. Our only place of blessing before God is among those whose highest joy is to confess that they are sinners saved by grace.

With Paul's fresh reminder of having sinned in the past, and his consciousness of being kept from sin daily, he was well aware of the power of sin that could overtake him without the daily presence and power of the indwelling Christ. "I know that nothing good lives in me" (Romans 7:18) describes the flesh as it is to the end. The glorious deliverance of Romans 8:2: "Through Christ Jesus the law of the Spirit of life set me free from the law of sin and death" is neither the annihilation nor the sanctification of the flesh, but a continuous victory given by the Spirit. As health expels disease, light swallows up darkness, and life conquers death, the indwelling Christ through the Spirit is the health, light, and life of the soul. But with this the conviction of helplessness tempers our faith with a sense of dependence that creates the proper humility in us and results in the greatest joy.

The passages above show that it was the wonderful grace bestowed upon Paul, of which he felt the need every moment, that humbled him so deeply. The grace of God that was with him and enabled him to labor more abundantly than they all, the grace to preach to the heathen the unsearchable riches of Christ, is what kept his sense of being liable to sin so alive. "But where sin increased, grace increased all the more" (Romans 5:20). This reveals how the very essence of grace deals with and takes away sin. The more abundant the experience of grace the more intense the consciousness of being a sinner. It is not sin, but God's grace showing a man and ever reminding him what a sinner he was that will keep him truly humble. It is not sin but grace that will make me know myself as a sinner.

I'm afraid that there are many who by strong expressions of self-condemnation and self-denunciation have sought to humble themselves, but who have to confess with sorrow that a humble spirit with its accompanying kindness and compassion, meekness and forbearance, is still as far off as ever. Being occupied with self, even having the deepest self-abhorrence, can never free us from self. It is the revelation of God not only by the law condemning sin but also by His grace delivering from it that will make us humble. The law may break the heart with fear; it is only grace that works that sweet humility that becomes joy to the soul as its second nature. It was the revelation of God in His holiness, drawing nigh to make himself known in His grace that made Abraham, Jacob, Job, and Isaiah bow so low. It is the soul that finds God to be everything that is so filled with His presence there is no place for self. So alone can the promise be fulfilled: "The pride of men brought low; the Lord alone will be exalted in that day" (Isaiah 2:11).

It is the sinner basking in the full light of God's holy, redeeming love, in the experience of that indwelling divine compassion of Christ, who cannot but be humble. Not to be occupied with your sin but to be fully occupied with God brings deliverance from self.

## chapter nine
# humility and faith

---

"Be not angry that you cannot make others as you
wish them to be, since you cannot make yourself
as you wish yourself to be."

THOMAS À KEMPIS

How can you believe if you accept praise from one another, yet make no effort to obtain the praise that comes from the only God?

**John 5:44**

In an address I heard recently, the speaker said that the blessings of the higher Christian life were often like the objects displayed in a shop window: one could see them clearly and yet could not reach them. If told to reach out and help himself, a man would answer, "I can't; there's a thick pane of plate glass between me and them." In the same way, Christians may see clearly the blessed promises of perfect peace and rest, overflowing love and joy, abiding communion and fruitfulness, and yet feel that there is something hindering their possession. What is it that hinders? The promises made to faith are free and sure; the invitation and encouragement strong; the mighty power of God close at hand and free. All that hinders the blessing being ours is pride or a lack of faith. In our text, Jesus reveals to us that it is indeed pride that makes faith impossible: "How can you believe if you accept praise from one another?" As we see how in their very nature pride and faith are irreconcilably at odds, we learn that faith and humility are at their root one, and that we can never have more of true faith than we have of true humility. It is possible to have strong intellectual convictions and assurance of the truth while pride is still in the heart, but it makes living faith, which has power with God, impossible.

We have only to think for a moment what faith is. Is it not a confession of helplessness, the surrender to God that waits to let Him work? Is it not in itself the most humbling thing there can be—the acceptance of our place as dependents who can claim, or get, or do nothing but what grace bestows? Humility is simply the disposition that prepares the soul for living in trust. Even the most secret breath of pride, in self-seeking, self-will, self-confidence, or self-exaltation, is only the strengthening of that self that cannot enter the kingdom or possess the things of the kingdom because it refuses to allow God to be who He is.

Faith is the means by which we perceive and apprehend the heavenly world and its blessings. Faith seeks the glory that comes when God is all. As long as we take glory from one another, as long as we seek and love and jealously guard the glory of this life, the honor and reputation that comes from men, we do not seek and cannot receive the glory that comes from God. Pride renders faith impossible. Salvation comes through the cross and the crucified Christ. Salvation is the fellowship with the crucified Christ in the Spirit of His cross. Salvation is union with and delight in, even participation in the humility of Jesus. Is it any wonder that our faith is weak when pride still reigns and we have hardly learned to long or pray for humility as the most necessary and blessed part of salvation?

Humility and faith are more nearly allied in Scripture than many realize. See it in the life of Christ. There are two cases in which He spoke of great faith. He marveled at the faith of the centurion, saying, "I have not found anyone in Israel with such great faith." The centurion had said, "Lord, I do not deserve to have you come under my roof" (Matthew 8:5–13). And the mother to whom He said, "It is not right to take the children's bread and toss it to their dogs," replied, "Yes, Lord, but even the dogs eat the crumbs." To her, he replied, "Woman, you have great faith! Your request is granted" (Matthew 15:22–28). It is humility that brings a soul to be nothing before God and that also removes every hindrance to faith and makes it only fear lest it dishonor Him by not trusting Him completely.

If there is failure in the pursuit of holiness, it most surely has pride and self at its root. We have no idea to what extent pride and self secretly work within us, or how God alone by His indwelling power can cast them out. Nothing but the new and divine nature taking the place of the old self can make us truly humble. Absolute, unceasing humility must be the core disposition of every prayer and approach to God as well as every relationship with our fellowmen.

We go to such lengths to believe, while the old self in its pride seeks to avail itself of God's blessing and riches. No wonder we can't believe. We need to change our course. We need to humble ourselves under the mighty hand of God: He will exalt us. The cross, death, and the grave, into which Jesus humbled himself, were His path to the glory of God. And they are our path too. Let humility be our one desire and our fervent prayer. Let us gladly accept whatever humbles us before God or men—this alone is the path to the glory of God.

I have spoken of some who have blessed experiences or are the means of bringing blessing to others and yet are lacking in humility. You may ask whether these do not prove that they have true, even strong faith, though they show all too clearly that they still seek the honor that comes from men. There is more than one answer to this. But the principal answer in our present connection is this: they have a measure of faith in proportion to the blessing they bring to others. But the real work of their faith is hindered through their lack of humility. The blessing is often superficial or transitory because they by their failure to be "nothing" block the way for God to be all. A deeper humility would bring a deeper and fuller blessing. The Holy Spirit, working in them not only as a Spirit of power but also dwelling in them in the fullness of His grace, and especially that of humility, would through them communicate himself to others a life of power and holiness and steadfastness as yet unseen.

"How can you believe if you accept praise from one another?" Nothing can cure you of the desire to receive glory from men or of the sensitiveness and pain and anger that come when it is not given, but seeking alone the glory that comes from God. Let the glory of the all-glorious God be everything to you. You will be freed from the glory of men and of self and be content and glad to be nothing. Out of this nothingness you will grow strong in faith, giving glory to God, and you will find that the deeper you sink in humility before Him, the nearer He is to fulfill every desire of your faith.

## chapter ten

# humility and death to self

---

"Humility is the most difficult of all virtues to achieve; nothing dies harder than the desire to think well of oneself."

T. S. ELIOT

He humbled himself and became obedient to death.

**Philippians 2:8**

Humility is the path to death, because in death it gives the highest proof of its perfection. Humility is the blossom of which death to self is the perfect fruit. Jesus humbled himself unto death and opened the path in which we too must walk. As there was no way for Him to prove His surrender to God to the uttermost or to give up and rise out of our human nature to the glory of the Father but through death, so it is with us. Humility must lead us to die to self: so we prove how wholly we have given ourselves up to it and to God; so alone we are freed from our fallen nature and find the path that leads to life in God, to that full birth of the new nature, of which humility is the breath and the joy.

We have spoken of what Jesus did for His disciples when He communicated His resurrection life to them, when in the descent of the Holy Spirit, glorified and enthroned meekness, He actually came from heaven himself to dwell in them. He won the power to do this through death: in its inmost nature, the life He imparted was a life out of death, a life that had been surrendered to death and been won through death. He who came to dwell in them was himself one who had been dead and lives forevermore. His life, His person, His presence, bears the marks of death, a life begotten out of death. That life in His disciples ever bears the marks of death too; it is only as the Spirit of the dying One dwells and works in the soul that the power of His life can be known. The first mark of the dying of the Lord Jesus—the mark that shows the true follower of Jesus—is humility. For these two reasons: only humility leads to perfect death; only death perfects humility. Humility and death are in their very nature one: humility is the bud; in death the fruit is ripened to perfection.

*Humility leads to perfect death.* Humility means giving up self, taking the place of perfect nothingness before God. Jesus humbled himself and became obedient unto death. In death He gave the highest and perfect proof of having given up His will to the will of God. In death He gave up self with its natural reluctance to drink the cup; He gave up the life He had in union with our human nature; He died to self and the sin that tempted Him; so, as man, He entered into the perfect life of God. If it had not been for His boundless humility, counting himself as nothing except as a servant to do and suffer the will of God, He never would have died.

This gives us the answer to the question so often asked and seldom clearly understood: How can I die to self? Death to self is not your work; it is God's work. In Christ *you are dead* to sin; your life has gone through the process of death and resurrection. But the full manifestation of the power of this death in your disposition and conduct depends upon the measure in which the Holy Spirit imparts the power of the death of Christ. And here it is that the teaching is needed: If you would enter into full fellowship with Christ in His death, and know the full deliverance from self, humble yourself. This is your duty. Place yourself before God in your helplessness; consent to the fact that you are powerless to slay yourself; give yourself in patient and trustful surrender to God. Accept every humiliation; look upon every person who tries or troubles you as a means of grace to humble you. God will see such acceptance as proof that your whole heart desires it. It is the path of humility that leads to the full and perfect experience of our death with Christ.

Beware of the mistake so many make. They have so many qualifications and limitations, so many thoughts and questions as to what true humility is to be and to do that they never unreservedly yield themselves to it. Humble yourself unto death. It is in the death to self that humility is perfected. At the root of all real experience of grace and true advance in consecration is conformity to the likeness of Jesus, which affects our dispositions and our habits. The reason I mention disposition and habit is that it is possible to speak of walking in the Spirit while there is still evidence of self. True humility will manifest itself in daily life. The one who has it will take the form of a servant. It is possible to speak of fellowship with a despised and rejected Jesus and of bearing His cross, while the meek and lowly Lamb of God is not seen and rarely sought. The Lamb of God means two things: meekness and death. Let us seek to receive Him in both forms.

What a hopeless task if we had to do the work ourselves! Nature never can overcome nature, not even with the help of grace. Self can never cast out self, even in the regenerate man. Praise God! The work has been done, finished, and perfected forever. The death of Jesus, once and for all, is our death to self. And the ascension of Jesus, His entering once and forever into the Holy of Holies, has given us the Holy Spirit to communicate to us with power. As the soul in the pursuit and practice of humility follows in the steps of Jesus, its consciousness of the need of something more is awakened, its desire and hope is quickened, its faith strengthened, and it learns to look up and claim that true fullness of the Spirit of Jesus that can daily maintain His death to self and sin in its full power and make humility the all-pervading spirit of our life.[1]

"Or don't you know that all of us who were baptized into Christ Jesus were *baptized into his death?* . . . Count yourselves *dead to sin* but alive to God in Christ Jesus. . . . Offer yourselves to God, as those who have been *brought from death to life*" (Romans 6:3, 11, 13). The whole self-awareness of the Christian is to be imbued by the spirit of the sacrifice of Christ. He must present himself to God as one who has died with Christ and in Christ is alive again. His life will bear the twofold mark: its roots in the humility of Jesus, death to sin and self; its head lifted up in resurrection power.

Claim in faith the death and the life of Jesus as your own. Enter into rest from self and its work—the rest of God. With Christ, who committed His spirit into the Father's hands, humble yourself and acknowledge each day your helpless dependence upon God. God will raise you up and exalt you. Every morning remind yourself afresh of your emptiness so that the life of Jesus may be manifested in you. Let a willing, loving, restful humility be the mark that you have claimed your birthright—the baptism into the death of Christ. "By one sacrifice he has made perfect forever those who are being made holy" (Hebrews 10:14). The souls that enter into *His* humiliation will find *in Him* the power to see and count self as dead and, as those who have learned and received of Him, to walk with all lowliness and meekness, forbearing one another in love.

## chapter eleven
# humility and happiness

---

"Should you ask me: What is the first thing in religion? I should reply: the first, second, and third thing therein is humility."

AUGUSTINE

Therefore I will boast all the more gladly about my weaknesses, so that Christ's power may rest on me. That is why, for Christ's sake, I delight in weaknesses. . . . For when I am weak, then I am strong.

2 Corinthians 12:9–10

It seems that Paul's thorn in the flesh was sent to humble him so that he might not exalt himself as a result of the great revelations given to him. Paul's first desire was to have the thorn removed, and he asked the Lord three times that it might be taken away. The answer came to him that the trial was a blessing—that through the weakness and humiliation it brought, the grace and strength of the Lord could better be manifested. Paul at once entered upon a new stage in his relationship to the trial: instead of simply enduring it, *he gladly gloried* in it; instead of asking for deliverance, *he took pleasure* in it. He had learned that the place of humiliation is the place of blessing, of power, and of joy.

Many Christians fear and flee and seek deliverance from all that would humble them. At times they may pray for humility, but in their heart of hearts they pray even more to be kept from the things that would bring them to that place. They have not reached the level of seeing humility as a manifestation of the beauty of the Lamb of God. There is still a sense of burden connected with humility in their minds; to humble themselves has not become the spontaneous expression of their lives.

Can we hope to reach the stage in which this will be the case? Certainly. By the same way that Paul reached it: a new revelation of the Lord Jesus. Nothing but the presence of God can reveal and expel self. A clearer insight was to be given to Paul into the deep truth that the presence of Jesus banishes every desire to seek anything in ourselves. It will make us delight in every humiliation that prepares us for His fuller manifestation.

We may know advanced believers, eminent teachers, and men of great spiritual experience who have not yet learned to embrace humility. We see this danger in Paul's situation. The inevitability of exalting himself was close at hand. He didn't yet know what it was to be nothing; to die, that Christ alone might live in him; to take pleasure in all that brought him low. It appears that this was the greatest lesson that he had to learn.

Every Christian who seeks to advance in holiness should remember this: there may be intense consecration and fervent zeal, and if the Lord himself does not step in, there may be unconscious self-exaltation. Let us learn the lesson that the greatest holiness comes in the deepest humility.

Let us look at our lives in the light of this experience and see whether we gladly glory in weakness, and whether we take pleasure, as Paul did, in injuries, in necessities, in distresses. Yes, let us ask whether we have learned to regard a reproof, just or unjust, a reproach from a friend or an enemy, an injury, or trouble, or difficulty as an opportunity for proving that Jesus is all to us. It is indeed the deepest happiness of heaven to be so free from self that whatever is said of us or done to us is swallowed up in the thought that Jesus is all and we are nothing.

Let us trust Him who took care of Paul to take care of us too. Paul needed special discipline, and with it special instruction to learn what was more precious than even the unutterable things he had heard from heaven: what it is to glory in weakness and lowliness. We need it too. The school in which Jesus taught Paul is our school as well. He watches over us with a jealous, loving care, lest we exalt ourselves. When we do this, He seeks to show to us the evil of it and to deliver us from it. Through trials and failures and troubles, He seeks to bring us to the place where His grace is everything. His strength is made perfect in our weakness; His presence fills and satisfies our emptiness; and becomes the secret of humility. Paul could say, "I am not in the least inferior to the 'super-apostles,' even though I am nothing" (2 Corinthians 12:11).

"I will boast all the more gladly about my weaknesses, so that Christ's power may rest on me" (2 Corinthians 12:9). The humble man has learned the secret of abiding joy. The weaker he feels, the lower he sinks, the greater his humiliations, the more the power and presence of Christ is his portion. When he says, "I am nothing," the word of his Lord comes: "My grace is sufficient for you" (2 Corinthians 12:9).

*The danger of pride is greater and nearer than we think,* and especially at the time of our greatest experiences. The preacher of spiritual truth with an admiring congregation hanging on his every word, the gifted speaker of a holiness convention expounding the secrets of the heavenly life, the Christian giving testimony to a blessed experience—no man knows the hidden, unconscious danger to which these are exposed. Paul was in danger without knowing it: what Jesus did for him is written for our admonition, that we may know our danger and know our only safety. If ever it has been said of a teacher or professor of holiness: he is so full of self; or he does not practice what he preaches; or his blessing has not made him humbler or gentler—let it be said no more. Jesus, in whom we trust, can make us humble.

*The grace for humility is also greater and nearer than we think.* The humility of Jesus is our salvation: Jesus himself is our humility. His grace is sufficient for us to meet the temptation of pride. His strength will be perfected in our weakness. Let us choose to be weak, to be low, to be nothing. Let humility be to us joy and gladness. Let us gladly glory and take pleasure in weakness, in all that will humble us and keep us low; the power of Christ will rest upon us. Christ humbled himself, therefore God exalted Him. Christ will humble us and keep us humble; let us heartily consent, let us trustfully and joyfully accept all that humbles; the power of Christ will rest upon us. We shall find that the deepest humility is the secret of the truest happiness, of a joy that nothing can destroy.

## chapter twelve
## humility and exaltation

---

"I used to think that God's gifts were on shelves—one above another—and the taller we grow, the easier we can reach them. Now I find that God's gifts are on shelves—and the lower we stoop, the more we get."

F. B. MEYER

He who humbles himself will be exalted.

Luke 14:11; 18:14

---

God ... gives grace to the humble.... Humble yourselves
before the Lord, and he will lift you up.

James 4:6, 10

---

Humble yourselves, therefore, under God's mighty hand, that
he may lift you up in due time.

1 Peter 5:6

Recently I was asked the question, "How can I overcome my pride?" The answer is simple. Two things are needed. Do what God says to do: humble yourself. Trust Him to do what He says He will do: He will exalt you.

The command is clear. But to humble yourself does not mean that you must conquer and cast out the pride of your nature and then form within yourself the lowliness of Jesus. No, this is God's work. He lifts you up into the true likeness of His beloved Son. What the command does mean is this: take every opportunity to humble yourself before God and man. In the faith of the grace that is already working in you; in the assurance of the grace for the victory that is yet to be; stand persistently under the unchanging command: humble yourself. Accept with gratitude everything that God allows from within or without, from friend or enemy, in nature or in grace, to remind you of your need for humbling and to help you in it. Reckon humility to be the mother-virtue, your very first duty before God, the one perpetual safeguard of the soul, and set your heart upon it as the source of all blessing. The promise is divine and sure: He that humbles himself shall be exalted. See that you do the one thing that God asks, and He will see that He does the one thing He has promised. He will give more grace; He will exalt you in due time.

All God's dealings with man are characterized by two stages. There is the time of preparation, when command and promise, with the mingled experience of effort and impotence, of failure and partial success, with the holy expectancy of something better, that these waken, train, and discipline men for a higher stage. Then comes the time of fulfillment, when faith inherits the promise and enjoys what it had so often struggled for in vain. This law holds good in every part of the Christian life and in the pursuit of every separate virtue. And that is because it is grounded in the very nature of things. In all that concerns our redemption, God must take the initiative. When that has been done, it is man's turn. In the effort after obedience and attainment, he must learn to know his power-lessness, in self-despair to die to himself, and so be fitted voluntarily and intelligently to receive from God the end, the completion of that which he had accepted in the beginning in ignorance. So God who had been the Beginning before man rightly knew Him or fully understood what His purpose was, is longed for and welcomed as the End, as the All in All.

It is so, too, in the pursuit of humility. To every Christian the command comes from the throne of God himself: humble yourself. The earnest attempt to listen and obey will be rewarded with the painful discovery of two things: the depth of our pride, and the powerlessness of all our efforts to destroy it. Blessed is the man who has learned to put his hope in God. We know the law of human nature: acts produce habits, habits breed dispositions, dispositions form the will, and the rightly formed will becomes the character. It is no different in the work of grace. As acts, persistently repeated, beget habits and dispositions, and these strengthen the will, He who works both to will and to do in us comes with His mighty power and Spirit; and the humbling of the proud heart with which the penitent saint so often casts himself before God is rewarded with the "more grace" of the humble heart.

Humble yourselves in the sight of the Lord, and He will exalt you. It cannot be repeated too often. The highest glory of the creature is in being a vessel, to receive and enjoy and show forth the glory of God. It can do this only as it is willing to be nothing in itself, that God may be everything. Water always fills first the lowest places. The lower, the emptier a man lies before God, the speedier and the fuller will be the inflow of the divine glory. The exaltation God promises is not, cannot be, any external thing apart from himself: all that He has to give or can give is only more of himself, in order that He might take the more complete possession. The exaltation is not, like an earthly prize, something arbitrary, in no connection with the conduct to be rewarded. It is in its very nature the effect and result of the humbling of ourselves. It is nothing but the gift of such a divine indwelling humility, such a conformity to and possession of the humility of the Lamb of God, as fits us for receiving fully the indwelling of God.

He that humbles himself shall be exalted. Of the truth of these words Jesus himself is the proof; of the certainty of their fulfillment to us He is the pledge. Let us take His yoke upon us and learn of Him, for He is meek and lowly of heart. If we are but willing to stoop to Him, as He has stooped to us, He will yet stoop to each one of us again, and we shall find ourselves not unequally yoked with Him. As we enter deeper into the fellowship of His humiliation—and either humble ourselves or bear the humbling of men—we can count upon the fact that the Spirit of His exaltation, "the Spirit of God and of glory," will rest upon us. The presence and the power of the glorified Christ will come to them that are of a humble spirit. When God can again have His rightful place in us, He will lift us up. Make His glory your motivation to humble yourself; He will make your glory His motivation to perfect your humility. As the all-pervading life of God possesses you, there will be nothing so natural or sweet as to be nothing, with no thought or wish for self, because all is occupied with Him. "I will boast all the more gladly about my weaknesses, so that Christ's power may rest on me" (2 Corinthians 12:9).

Have we not here the reason that our consecration and our faith have availed so little in the pursuit of holiness? It was by self and its strength that the work was done under the name of faith; it was for self and its happiness that God was called in; it was, unconsciously, but still truly, in self and its holiness that the soul rejoiced. We never knew that humility—absolute, abiding, Christ-like humility—and self-effacement, pervading and marking our whole life with God and man, was the most essential element of the life of holiness for which we sought.

It is only in the possession of God that I lose myself. As it is in the height and breadth and glory of the sunshine that the smallest speck dancing in its beams is seen, even so humility is taking our place in God's presence to be nothing but a speck dancing in the sunlight of His love.

How great is God! How small we are! Lost, swallowed up, in love's immensity!

May God teach us to believe that to be humble, to be nothing in His presence, is the highest attainment and the fullest blessing of the Christian life. He speaks to us: "I live in a high and holy place, but also with him who is contrite and lowly in spirit" (Isaiah 57:15).

> Oh, to be emptier, lowlier,
> Mean, unnoticed, and unknown,
> And to God a vessel holier,
> Filled with Christ, and Christ alone!

# a prayer for humility

---

*The secret of secrets: humility is the soul of true prayer.* Until the spirit of the heart is renewed, until it is emptied of all earthly desires and stands in a habitual hunger and thirst after God, which is the true spirit of prayer; until then, all our prayer will be more or less like lessons given to students. We will mostly say them only because we dare not neglect them. But be not discouraged; take the following advice, and then you may go to church without any danger of mere lip-service or hypocrisy, although there may be a hymn or a prayer whose language is higher than that of your heart. Go to the church as the tax collector went to the temple; stand inwardly, in the spirit of your mind, in that form that he outwardly expressed when he cast down his eyes and could only say, "God be merciful to me, a sinner." Stand unchangeably, at least in your desire, in this form or state of heart; it will sanctify every petition that comes out of your mouth; and when anything is read or sung or prayed that is more exalted than your heart is, if you make this an occasion of further identifying with the spirit of the tax collector, you will then be helped and highly blessed by those prayers and praises that seem to belong to a heart better than yours.

This, my friend, is the secret of secrets. It will help you to reap where you have not sown and will be a continual source of grace in your soul; for everything that inwardly stirs you or outwardly happens to you becomes good to you if it finds you in this humble state of mind. For nothing is in vain or without profit to *the humble soul*; it stands always in a state of divine growth, and everything that falls upon it is like dew from heaven. Close yourself, therefore, in this form of humility; all good is enclosed in it; it is a fresh spring from heaven that turns the fire of the fallen soul into the meekness of the divine life, and creates that oil out of which the love to God and man gets its flame. Be always clothed in it; let it be as a garment wherewith you are always covered and a shield with which you are girded; breathe nothing but in and from its spirit; see nothing but with its eyes; hear nothing but with its ears. And then, whether you are in the church or out of the church, hearing the praises of God or receiving wrongs from men and the world, all will be edification, and everything will help promote your growth in the life of God.

I will here give you an infallible touchstone that will test all to the truth: retire from the world and all conversation for one month. Neither write, nor read, nor debate anything with yourself; stop all the former workings of your heart and mind, and with all the strength of your heart stand as continually as you can in the following form of prayer to God. Offer it frequently on your knees; but whether sitting, walking, or standing, be always inwardly longing and earnestly praying this one prayer to God: that of His great goodness He would make known to you, and take from your heart every kind and form and degree of pride, whether it be from evil spirits or your own corrupt nature; and that He would awaken in you the deepest depth and truth of that humility which can make you capable of His light and Holy Spirit. Reject every thought but that of waiting and praying in this manner from the bottom of your heart—with such truth and earnestness as people in agony pray and be delivered from their torment. In this spirit of prayer, I will venture to affirm that if you had twice as many evil spirits in you as Mary Magdalene had, they would all be cast out of you, and you would be forced with her to weep tears of love at the feet of the holy Jesus. (Adapted from *The Spirit of Prayer*, part 2, 121, 124, n.d.)

# notes

**Chapter One**

1. "All this to make it known through the region of eternity
that *pride* can degrade the highest angels into devils, and
*humility* can raise fallen flesh and blood to the thrones of
angels. This is the great end of God: raising a new creation
out of a fallen kingdom of angels; for this end it stands in
its state of war between the fire and pride of fallen angels
and the humility of the Lamb of God—that the last trum-
pet may sound the great truth through the depths of eternity that evil can have no beginning but from pride and no
end but from humility.

   "The truth is this: Pride must die in you or nothing of
heaven can live in you. Under the banner of the truth, give
yourself up to the meek and humble spirit of the holy Jesus.

Humility must sow the seed or there can be no reaping in heaven. Look not at pride only as an unbecoming temper, nor at humility only as a decent virtue: for the one is death and the other is life; the one is hell and the other is heaven. So much as you have of pride within you, you have of the fallen angel alive in you; so much as you have of true humility, so much you have of the Lamb of God within you.

"If you could see what every stirring of pride does to your soul, you would beg of everyone you meet to tear the viper from you, though with the loss of a hand or an eye. If you could see what a sweet, divine, transforming power there is in humility, how it expels the poison of your nature, and makes room for the Spirit of God to live in you, you would rather wish to be the footstool of all the world than want the smallest degree of it." Taken from *The Spirit of Prayer*, edition of Moreton, Canterbury, 1893, part 2, 73.


## Chapter Two

1. "We need to know two things: (1) Our salvation consists wholly in being saved from *ourselves*, or that which we are by nature; (2) In the whole nature of things, nothing could be salvation or savior to us but the humility of God beyond all expression. Hence the first unalterable term of 'Savior' of fallen man: 'Except a man deny himself he cannot be my disciple.' Self is the whole evil of the fallen nature. Self-denial is our capacity for being saved. Humility is our savior. . . . Self is the root, the branches, the tree, of all the evil of our fallen state. All the evil of fallen angels and of men

has its birth in the pride of self. On the other hand, all the virtues of the heavenly life stem from humility. It is humility alone that makes the impassable gulf between heaven and hell. What is then, or in what lies, the great struggle for eternal life? It all lies in the strife between pride and humility. Pride and humility are the two master powers, the two kingdoms at war for the eternal possession of man. There never was or ever will be but one humility, and that is the humility of Christ. Pride and self have the "all" of man, until man has his all in Christ. He only fights the good fight whose desire is that the self-idolatrous nature that he has from Adam may be put to death by the supernatural humility of Christ brought to life in him." Adapted from William Law, *Address to the Clergy*, n.d., 52.

## Chapter Ten

1. "To die to self, or come from under its power, is not, cannot, be done by any active resistance we can make to it by the powers of nature. The one true way of dying to self is the way of patience, meekness, humility, and resignation to God. If I ask you what the Lamb of God means, would you not tell me that it means the perfection of patience, meekness, humility, and resignation to God? Would you say that a desire for these virtues is a desire to give yourself up to Him? Because this inclination of your heart is to seek patience, meekness, humility, and resignation to God, giving up all that you are and all that you have is your highest act of faith in Him. Christ is nowhere but in these virtues;

when they are there, He is in His own kingdom. Let this be the Christ you follow.

"The Spirit of divine love can have no birth in any fallen creature till it wills and chooses to be dead to all self, in patient, humble resignation to the power and mercy of God.

"I seek for all my salvation through the merits and mediation of the meek, humble, patient, suffering Lamb of God, who alone hath power to bring forth the blessed birth of these heavenly virtues in my soul. There is no possibility of salvation but in and by the birth of the meek, humble, patient, resigned Lamb of God in our souls. When the Lamb of God has brought forth a real birth of His own meekness, humility, and full resignation to God in our souls, then it is the birthday of the Spirit of love in our souls, which, whenever we attain it, will feast our soul with such peace and joy in God as will blot out the remembrance of everything that we called peace or joy before.

"This way to God is infallible. This infallibility is grounded in the twofold character of our Savior: (1) As He is the Lamb of God, it is a principle of meekness and humility in the soul; (2) As He is the Light of heaven, and blesses eternal nature and turns it into a kingdom of heaven when we are willing to get rest for our soul in meek, humble resignation to God, then it is that He, as the Light of God and heaven, joyfully breaks in upon us, turns our darkness into light, and begins that kingdom of God and of love within us that will never have an end." Taken from William Law, *Dying to Self: A Golden Dialogue*, n.d.

*Thank you for selecting a book from*
BETHANY HOUSE PUBLISHERS

Bethany House Publishers is a ministry of Bethany
Fellowship International, an interdenominational,
nonprofit organization committed to spreading the
Good News of Jesus Christ around the world through
evangelism, church planting, literature distribution, and
care for those in need. Missionary training is offered
through Bethany College of Missions.

Bethany Fellowship International is a member of the
National Association of Evangelicals and subscribes to
its statement of faith. If you would like further
information, please contact:

Bethany Fellowship International
6820 Auto Club Road
Minneapolis, MN 55438 USA

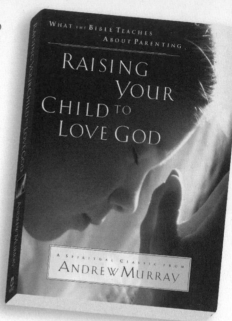